A Collection Of Imaginative Words

Edited By Lynsey Evans

First published in Great Britain in 2024 by:

Young Writers
Remus House
Coltsfoot Drive
Peterborough
PE2 9BF
Telephone: 01733 890066
Website: www.youngwriters.co.uk

All Rights Reserved
Book Design by Ashley Janson
© Copyright Contributors 2024
Softback ISBN 978-1-83565-810-9
Printed and bound in the UK by BookPrintingUK
Website: www.bookprintinguk.com
YB0606X

FOREWORD

Welcome Reader, to a world of dreams.

For Young Writers' latest competition, we asked our writers to dig deep into their imagination and create a poem that paints a picture of what they dream of, whether it's a make-believe world full of wonder or their aspirations for the future.

The result is this collection of fantastic poetic verse that covers a whole host of different topics. Let your mind fly away with the fairies to explore the sweet joy of candy lands, join in with a game of fantasy football, or you may even catch a glimpse of a unicorn or another mythical creature. Beware though, because even dreamland has dark corners, so you may turn a page and walk into a nightmare!

Whereas the majority of our writers chose to stick to a free verse style, others gave themselves the challenge of other techniques such as acrostics and rhyming couplets. We also gave the writers the option to compose their ideas in a story, so watch out for those narrative pieces too!

Each piece in this collection shows the writers' dedication and imagination – we truly believe that seeing their work in print gives them a well-deserved boost of pride, and inspires them to keep writing, so we hope to see more of their work in the future!

CONTENTS

Hart Plain Junior School, Waterlooville

Anna Thompson (9)	69
Oliver James (9)	70
Sofia Gisby (9)	71
Flora Haastrup (8)	72
Scarlett-Rose Downer (8)	73
Phoebe Kramer (9)	74

Lea Forest Primary Academy, Kitts Green

Usman Samaiga (8)	75
Georgia Payal (8)	76
Khizer Ali (10)	78
Maria Bibi (10)	80
Imarah Uddin (7)	81
Zara Alam (8)	82
Tamsin Dumitrascu (7)	83
Kayden Coates (9)	84
Mariam Iqbal Ali (9)	85
Aizah Waqas (8)	86
Esme Matthews (10)	87
Khadijah Love (10)	88
Zahra Balić (7)	89
Charlie Stretton-Yeomans (8)	90
Neo Montaque (8)	91
Amelia Caines (8)	92
Haniya Abbas (9)	93
Dominic Flynn (8)	94
Anaya Arshad (10)	95
George McLaughlin (8)	96
Inshrah Butt (9)	97
Maisie Tighe (9)	98
Alina Barak (8)	99

Staynor Hall Community Primary Academy, Selby

Mara O'Sullivan Candela (9)	100
Madelyn Simpson (7)	102
Jordan Banton (7)	104
Abigail Graham (8)	106

Esme Cleary (7)	108
Maya Ritchie (8)	109
Harper Jackson (9)	110
Áine Ritchie (8)	111
Katelyn Watson-Frank (9)	112
Sofia Hammill (9)	114
Leo Chambers (7)	115
Reid Reclusado (8)	116
Finlay Lawrence (9)	117
Isabelle Fitch (9)	118
Ruby Turnbull (9)	119
Bridget Thornton (8)	120
Leela Snowdon (8)	121
Layla Grace Cleary (9)	122
Poppy Roberts (8)	123
Joshua Bradshaw (8)	124
Harrison Boland (9)	125
Oliver Lees (8)	126
Oscar Chambers (9)	127
Philip Arrighi (8)	128
Noah Seagrave (8)	129
Joshua Terry (9)	130
Marceline Lindley (8)	131
Jessica Chambers (8)	132
Vienna Burgos-Crossley (8)	133
Theo Bailey (8)	134
Cariad Krysiak (8)	135
Elliot Shaw (8)	136
Harry Renshaw (7)	137
Sebastian Lee (8)	138
Isabella McCormack (7)	139
Patrick Mobbs (8)	140
William Curtis (7)	141
Lolah Ascough (9)	142
Max Speight (8)	143
Ruby Vincent (8)	144
Toby Hammill (8)	145
James Stokoe (9)	146
Kasper Foster (7)	147
Harry Fisher (9)	148
Macauley Pulleyn (8)	149
William Challis (9)	150
Harrison Lister (9)	151

Arabella Bradshaw (9)   152

Victory Primary School, Portsmouth

Oliver Keen (9)	153
Avery Herridge (10)	154
Hannah Aarons (10)	156
Diana Lacey (10)	157
Chase Britton (10)	158
Scarlett Page (10)	159
Isla Chappell (10)	160
Ivy Belle Lewis (9)	161
Lenny Bull (10)	162
Alfie Brown (10)	163
Joshua Irons (10)	164
Piper Hartley (10)	165
Elise East (9)	166
Cody Jenkins (10)	167
Riley Duffett (10)	168
Miguel Senobua (10)	169
Poppy McMillan (10)	170
Amelia Ellis (10)	171
Eli Hollis (10)	172
Taiten-Ray Holden (10)	173
Sebastian Marsh (9)	174
Calum Smith (10)	175
Lilly Barton (10)	176
Eva Udy (10)	177
Jayden Nutland (9)	178
George Jeune (9)	179

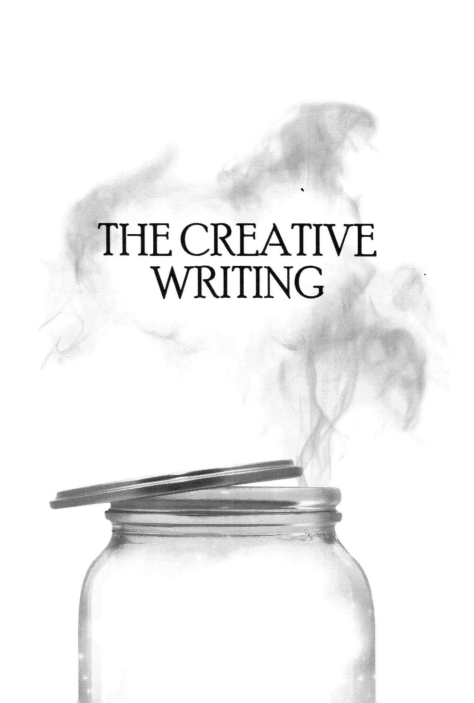

THE CREATIVE
WRITING

My Nightmare Came True!

I fell asleep in my living room at 3am,
Strangely I woke up in a dark house at 4am,
I heard a sound in a room,
I walked into the room and I saw something,
It was a monster holding a doll,
I thought it was a statue but it was a real monster.

I found a note on the floor, it said that I had to escape
from the house!
I ran to the door, it was locked,
I remembered that the back door had something to
unlock,
Nervously I found a note on the door, it was saying
look for some keys, I found them!
It was in order of the rainbow colours.

I found all the keys, I heard a noise behind me,
It was the monster with the doll!
I put the keys in order,
I woke up and I looked to the side,
And it was the monster and the doll!

Lara Ribeiro (9)
Button Lane Primary School, Wythenshawe

A Person In Deep Red

Once, I was at a club, the room had people cheering
and dancing
But this happened...
I woke up light-headed, the room was full of foam
The bed was as soft as cotton candy
The light was as loud as a volcano
As I explored, I felt a huge energy behind me,
As I kept on exploring, I felt strange,
I walked down the stairs, they had a cryptic sound as I
kept walking
When I finally went to the downstairs bathroom,
I was brushing my teeth
I saw the toothbrush made out of reddish substance
I immediately fled
In the city, the moon had a cheesy grin
And snow crunched under my feet
Until a man in deep red clothes had a black and blue
aura
Getting larger and larger
I had a fright which I tried to fight
When I closed my eyes, I was in a void with instinctive
energy flowing in and out
I was flying like fluffy cotton candy

As I closed my eyes, I fell on Earth
I was frightened thinking, *is this a dream or nightmare?*
And I woke up sweating drastically.

Faisal Awudu Adamu (9)
Button Lane Primary School, Wythenshawe

The Round Circus Dream!

As soon as I slept, I felt so tired.
The sky was pink then I looked, it was a circus.
A cloud was as fluffy as cotton candy.
The chocolate stand was made by chocolate,
It was as sweet as melted toffee sweets.

The circus had lots of people, it was like a maze!
That was when I wandered around the circus,
Trying to find some money that had dropped off the
floor.
A person approaching me handed me a cotton candy.
Two minutes passed, I sneaked away but then I
bumped into a kid,
Who was a toddler wearing a red T-shirt with a brown
shirt.

Then, as soon as I heard a beeping sound,
I closed my eyes then I was in the middle of a cloud!
Cotton candy spinning around and I crunched a bit of
my cotton candy,
It was as sweet as melted caramel on top of a waffle!
But the spinning cotton candy went on and on forever,

When I opened my eyes, I felt that I was in a horror movie.
Sadly, it was a dream and then I sat here doing nothing.

Ho Si Daniela Li (9)
Button Lane Primary School, Wythenshawe

Above The Clouds

Adventures are fun,
But sometimes it cuts,
On and up on clouds,
Violet clouds, pink clouds, blue clouds,
Eat all you want,
Could you count how many foods you ate?
Late at night, you sleep in bed,
Or jump on clouds with your friends,
Under the clouds, you are still dreaming,
Do you think it is fun up there?

Adventures are fun,
But sometimes it cuts,
On my bed, it felt as soft as candyfloss,
"Violet candyfloss?" I said,
Eat all the candy I want?
The house was made out of chocolate and toffee,
Haribos were everywhere,
Easy but hard to jump on,
Could I eat everything on the house?
Laughing and swimming in sweets,

As the popcorn popped out of the pan,
Under the candyfloss, I'm back in bed,
Dreaming back into bed, so disappointed.

Amelia Chobe (9)
Button Lane Primary School, Wythenshawe

Once Upon A Dream

I met Ella Toone!
Her team was losing which was a boom!
They were so close to scoring!
But Chelsea cheering was so boring.
When the first half was done, all of their faces were red like tomatoes.
When the second half came, I was so bored
That I would probably do a trick with a cord.
Man United came on, all the fans cheered.
Some Chelsea fans didn't
Although the food was yummy
I nearly threw up but I kept it in my tummy
Mary Earps is so great
You can't stop her and she won't break
Nikita Parris is my mum's favourite
She even signed my United shirt!
Which had a tiny bit of dirt.
Lauren James is really fast.
I can't believe she didn't trip in the past!

Jessica Howard (9)
Button Lane Primary School, Wythenshawe

Space Adventure

I open my eyes,
I feel like I'm enclosed in a space,
I'm on my back,
My body feels whack,
The ground starts to shake,
Is it an earthquake?
My eyes feel heavy,
I'm running out of air!
I look out at my golden hair,
I scream and use all my might, but I can't get up!
Then zip! Everything goes black,
I wake up to my mum in a spacesuit carrying me on her back,
I sit down to see women who tell me we're going to Mars!
We are going to live there,
My stuff is already there,
We get there - me, my mum and my teddy, of course,
When another spaceship whooshes past,
With my baby brother inside,
What an adventure me and Tiggy are having!

Laceyjo O'Neill (9)
Button Lane Primary School, Wythenshawe

The Magic Basketball

I woke up, got dressed and picked up my basketball
But something felt odd about it, but I didn't mind
When I got to the park, I shot the ball in the hoop
But when I scored it transformed into a football
When I scored the football in the net, it turned into a
basketball!
And if I kicked the basketball in the net, it screamed,
"Stop!"

I was amazed, it was a magic basketball
And it was as light as candyfloss!
But when I shot in the net, it whooshed
And hit the ground.
It went in the net and it shouted, "Wake up!"
And I woke up from my dream and got ready for
school.

Oliver Rowe (9)
Button Lane Primary School, Wythenshawe

The Enchanted World

I see a strange land,
There is no sand,
I am with my brother,
Suddenly I hear a slither,
It is coming towards us,
But we don't make a fuss,
We take a step behind
But there is nothing to find like a precious mind,
We blink. How? *Pop!* No snake!
I feel a snowflake,
And then I see a rabbit,
We take a step forward bit by bit,
The rabbit throws us its yo-yo,
And says, "Po-po,"
We don't understand it,
It has a yo-yo kit,
We ask if it could send us away,
But it wants to play,
Although we arrive home
Near our front door is a missing gnome!

Sujana Jawahar (8)
Button Lane Primary School, Wythenshawe

The Football Miracle

I'm a footballer,
And my team is losing.
What can I do?
Substitution, Bruno off, Ryley on.
Ryley is having a strong performance.
Ryley has a chance, he runs like Usain Bolt.
He shoots, he scores, it goes in!
Crowd goes wild.
Ryley has scored his first shot of the game.
Half-time at the chocolate fountain arena - second half
commences.
With Ryley rocking the midfield.
The team loves Ryley - even the manager.
Ryley always passes and shoots if necessary.
The crowd always goes wild.
Ryley shoots, he hits the post.
VAR goal, he wins it for United,
At the Chocolate Arena.

Ryley Cosgrove (9)
Button Lane Primary School, Wythenshawe

Darkness Turns To Light

I wake up in a field of poppies,
I feel petrified or scared,
My dog starts to bark,
It is dark,
I'm wondering if I'm safe,
The sky is as dark as a black car in the shadows,
It is warm and cosy,
A strange man walks up to me,
This man has a pink beard and a bright blue hat.
He grabs my hand,
He tells me to walk with him,
"Am I safe?" I ask myself,
We enter a portal,
He takes me to a place,
A place called the City of Wonderment!
Anything you wish for comes true,
But then I realised light will always beat darkness.
Darkness always turns to light.

Isabella Sudlow (9)
Button Lane Primary School, Wythenshawe

Sweetworld

I woke up in a room full of sweets,
The mattress was medium-sized,
The bed was made out of pink chocolate,
I found out the pillow was made from candyfloss,
That was as soft as a cloud.

I got out of bed to brush my teeth,
But the toothpaste was made out of chocolate,
Suddenly, there was a loud *bang!*
A car magically appeared,
The car roared at the stormy sky.

I went outside to drive the car,
The car seats were as blue as the sky,
It was magnificent! I pinched myself and
Found myself in my own bed on Earth,
I was super disappointed.

Veronica Njame (9)
Button Lane Primary School, Wythenshawe

The Never-Ending Road

At night, I lay in my bed and I closed my eyes.
Suddenly, I found myself in a different universe.
I walked and walked as the bright moon shone as much as it could.
The house was the same and after a day, my legs started to hurt so I sat down on the curb.

When I sat down, I instantly felt way better so I kept walking.
It seemed like I was in a loop but I didn't know,
After one hour, my legs started to hurt again,
When I sat down, I suddenly teleported to an alternate dimension
Then I woke up in real life,
I whooshed up from my bed
It was a nightmare.

Blake Harley Cooper (9)
Button Lane Primary School, Wythenshawe

Unicorn Academy

Some unicorns were sparkling like stars in the sky,
The academy looked beautiful with decorations,
The beds were alive and were as comfy and fluffy as clouds,
The clouds were rainbows,

The stars were sparkling but the unicorns were brighter,
Some academy unicorn riders also had wands that worked,
The unicorns were as beautiful as the sunshine,
Some unicorns could fly like a spacecraft.

The academy unicorns had special powers,
Some unicorns had different elemental powers,
The grass was as green as emeralds,
Trees were as green as emeralds.

Richard Babafemi (9)
Button Lane Primary School, Wythenshawe

Monstrous Monsters

Ha, finally we were here on the gigantic moon.
Eventually, all the brightest colours filled my head.
"Who are you?" I said.
They said, "What kind of language is that?"
My starved belly rumbled, rumbled
"Yes," I said. A biscuit.
They gazed at me with awesome eyes.
They pulled out a slime machine, argh run!
They got me in mid-air,
Crash! Bang! Wallop!
They got a biscuit!
They put me in a sack with all black and got me out.
I went back in my ship to Earth.
I woke up in my bed.
It was nothing real.

Harry Hough (8)
Button Lane Primary School, Wythenshawe

My Nightmare But What To Do

I dreamt of,
A scary memory,
I never want to go back,
Never, never go back,
Your nightmare - so don't share,
You might fight,
Or you may walk back,
But you may fight back,
So be prepared for what may come your way,
But it will stay in your head,
It will be scary,
No one likes a nightmare,
Even not me,
It will scare you but don't be afraid,
If you can, try to wake,
So always be brave,
Always suffer,
You are not the only person,
It is like walking up a hill,
Then down,
But suffering from heat.

Brooke Burrows (9)
Button Lane Primary School, Wythenshawe

Once Upon A Dream

I drifted off to sleep,
Sleep in a magical sea
Where mermaids have a secret entrance

A hole in a rock
A hole that leads to a gorgeous bridge
A bridge they swim across
Swim to a magical moon pool
Where their past wish came true
Their wish once upon a time
Was to be a magical mermaid
Once upon a time
When they were humans
Like me and you
I stood at the edge of the moon pool
Where the tree mermaids swam
Showing off their beauty
Rainbow scales
And powers of steam
And levitation.

Summer Atkinson (8)
Button Lane Primary School, Wythenshawe

Once Upon A Time

A dream with spiders and monsters,
Someone under the bed pulling your legs,
Fire spreading around the house, burning alive,
Being thrashed by a dragon breathing fire,
Falling into a hole leading to death,
Getting hanged by the head,
Going into a haunted school seeing clowns,
A big furry monster chasing you,
Getting out of breath and collapsing,
Spiders and snakes on your face,
Tornado sirens as loud as motorbikes,
Fish biting your legs,
Blood to write as lead in a pen,
Zombie apocalypse siren is spreading all over.

Isla Rae Myers-Shaw (9)
Button Lane Primary School, Wythenshawe

Once Upon A Dream

There was an Xbox walking towards the cat bed.
Once they met, they walked to the arcade.
Once they got there, something strange happened.
A war started, Nerf World War Three, now in
Manchester!
Two teams with three people on one side.
I didn't expect them to fight at all.
The next day, they threw a party and it was illegal. And
they got beer for tomorrow.
They ran a school, not a random, it's one where United
played.
It was a miracle! A new player AJR (Me, I played and I
scored forty goals in one game.)

Aurthur Harrop (9)
Button Lane Primary School, Wythenshawe

The Small Day

My grandpa turned off my light to get to bed in the
darkness,
I pulled my blanket up to sleep with a loud creak, my
door closed and my grandpa left,
I got scared because the darkness, slowly like a virus,
overcame my room,
I lay on my soft as cotton pillows,

I then felt more cold and I could hear woodland
animals so I got up and started exploring,
I was the only human then I got excited because there
were no prices and everything was open but when I
went to wash my face,
I sadly woke up, scared again in the night.

Noah Hagan (9)
Button Lane Primary School, Wythenshawe

Once Upon A Dream

I was putting my washing away
When my shoe came alive!
It ran upstairs and downstairs,
Along the road, faster and faster
Shop after shop it went
Into a posh hotel
Like lightning they went
Oh! What a dream!

I ran as fast as a flash,
I caught up with the shoes
They tried to run away again
But I tied the laces tight together
They could not move

I took them home
And put them in the wash.
They do not like the spinning washing machine.

Ready to run another day.

Isaiah Walters (8)
Button Lane Primary School, Wythenshawe

The Best Dream Ever

I was in a town, a town that was filled with dreams.
The town was filled with love hearts.
All the birds were cheeping loudly.
My mum didn't know where we were
Neither did my brother
But I did.
We were in Love Land.
I was so happy, I was with my family.
My mum had a surprise for me.
My mum said we were staying for a day.
My tummy started to tingle.
I filled with excitement.
"Thank you, oh thank you, Mum"
But now, I wake up and find myself in bed!

Kacey Robbins (9)
Button Lane Primary School, Wythenshawe

A Christmas Dream

One Christmas I thought I'd wake up,
To my mum's hot chocolate,
Filled to the brim,
With marshmallows and cookies,
Marshmallow soft pink and fluffy
Like lots of summer clouds.

I floated on a marshmallow,
Into my living room,
Dad was sitting in a big coffee mug,
Sipping and swimming
In the coffee inside!

Mum jumped on the ride,
We floated for a while,
As she passed me my Christmas gift,
How did she fit my bike inside?

Jackson Houghton (9)
Button Lane Primary School, Wythenshawe

Once Upon A Dream

Last night, I had a dream,
Warm, creamy hot chocolate milk,
The best I'd ever seen.
It tantalised my taste buds,
And not scared of my bad dreams.

A world where everything is perfect,
Houses made of cotton candy
And all types of caramel.
Children were so happy
And the parents were as well!

I love that place of dreams,
Where everything is great.
Where I felt safe and happy
And no one is scared.

Jewel Shilo (9)
Button Lane Primary School, Wythenshawe

My Toys Came Alive

I was in my room
It was as messy as a bin
But I was too lazy to clean it
I wanted to play
But it was way too messy
So I went to go lay down when suddenly
Crash! Bang! I got up from bed to check
What! I saw all my toys alive
I was so happy because now I can play with them
But they were not happy
They were angry.
They all came running on me
And I quickly cleaned up my room
And it never happened again.

Aimen Waqas (9)
Button Lane Primary School, Wythenshawe

Nightmares At The School

Yesterday, I went,
To an awful school!
They gave a large amount of calculations,
That even a calculator couldn't do!
There were souls like wisps of clouds
Flew around the classroom,
Spider shot webs
From all eight legs
And the teachers were vampires

Lying around on the broken floor,
Were skeletons in the river of blood.
Bats flying overhead
Be careful not to fall,
Into the world of dark death!

Nihal Shakavas (9)
Button Lane Primary School, Wythenshawe

The Beach And Sea

The sea on the beach is a wonderful sea.
You can swim in it as long as you want.
I love all the animals that live in the water.
They are so cute because, when you look at turtles,
they have a cute face when looking at you.
My dog, mum, dad, sister and my little boy called Samy
were at the beach.
Everyone loves the beach so much.
I feel very happy, sad and excited.
The kids love to play at the beach. They say it's lovely.

Mira Lee (8)
Button Lane Primary School, Wythenshawe

Once Upon A Dream

I will pass Mr Beast in subscribers and get 500 million subscribers,
I skyrocketed from 26 subscribers to 52k subscribers in one week,
I will do challenges and giveaways in my videos,
I get a 500 million custom play button for being the first YouTuber to get 500 million.
I will give away my 700 million play button when I get seven billion subscribers.
In my dreams, I get a world record for the most-liked video in history.

Lucas Hays (9)
Button Lane Primary School, Wythenshawe

Candyland

I woke up and found out I was on a chocolate and marshmallow bed. Then I looked out of the window, everything was candy. I was in Candyland and Lucas was outside, he said it was a miracle, so I also went outside.

Then after a bit, I was out of energy, so I ate some of the toffee. After that, I raced Lucas and won. But after the race, we were both super tired and out of energy. So we went to our house and got into bed and we both fell asleep.

Henry Hume (8)
Button Lane Primary School, Wythenshawe

The Missing Ball

We were playing with the ball
Then someone came over and started playing.
We didn't like him.
When he was leaving, he took the ball with him
And started to run.
The big ball was as light as candyfloss.
He fell over with a boom!
I wondered, *did it hurt?*
He said, "Ow! It did hurt."
We got the ball that felt like candyfloss.
He went and we started playing again.

Jack Taylor (8)
Button Lane Primary School, Wythenshawe

Nightmare Of Clowns

On a stormy night, there was a haunted house.
In the window peeked a scary figure, it was a clown!
It was smiling at me!
I opened the door, I saw a-a-a *demon!*
The door behind me slammed shut,
I started to shake!
I ran upstairs but there was the clown!
It came running at me!
As I closed the door, I woke up
I was back in my room but
Wait!
What was that scary noise?

Enmanuel Minyety (9)
Button Lane Primary School, Wythenshawe

Once Upon A Dream

Dream team time
Rashford, fast as a jaguar
More skilled than most players
Phil Foden, a blue streak of electric spark
Sweeps past the defenders
Goal!
Kevin, flame-haired with outstanding assists
His boots on fire!
Doku, drives past all of the midfield
And shoots like a bullet
Ederson, furious, unstoppable goalkeeper
Powerful kicks and tough hands.

Zack Williams (9)
Button Lane Primary School, Wythenshawe

Love Nightmare

Your nightmares are like real life.
They give you a fright in the night.
In the day, they stay away
When they come, do not run

Loving nightmares aren't as cosy as a blanket.
Whooo! Boo!
The love monster said
"I will kill you! Haha pranked you."

When they love you
They buy a gift for you.
If they die
Do not cry.

Jamar Hylton (9)
Button Lane Primary School, Wythenshawe

In The Dark

I woke up and I was at a park,
There were lots of bright lights surrounding a pier.
There was a black figure on the pier!
Then I looked to my left and a man was running at me!
He chased me until midday, I stopped,
I thought I lost him.
I looked to my right and I saw him,
I ran and he walked away,
He disappeared into the darkness.

Isabella James (9)
Button Lane Primary School, Wythenshawe

My Dream House

There was obsidian for the door
And diamonds for the walls
Sparkly crystals for the windows

Flowers rising
Wonderful flowers from the glorious Earth
Beauty everywhere

Long, tall trees
As tall as a lamp post, straight as a stamp,
Lamp post, as huge as a skyscraper
Lamp post, as bright as a car's headlights.

Harry Wakefield (9)
Button Lane Primary School, Wythenshawe

Once Upon A Dream

I can enter a world where I have a trillion pounds
I wish I had an exotic car
I dream I have a famous chef and cleaner
I dream and wish I was a famous footballer
A golden retriever as a pet - I wish!
I dream I live in a mega-mansion - as high as the sky.
With a swimming pool in my backyard
I wish, I wish, I wish all of the time.

Jacob Appleton (9)
Button Lane Primary School, Wythenshawe

The Sleepover

I went to my friend's sleepover and on the way, I rang the bell,
When I came inside the house, I saw her with her kind parents,
As I came walking upstairs to check out her room,
It was as blue as the sky,
She wanted her hair to be dyed the colours of the rainbow,
Purple, red, blue and yellow.
Suddenly, I was woken by a loud bang!

Lavinia Tafriengika (8)
Button Lane Primary School, Wythenshawe

Clowns Nightmare

The clowns circle me in horror,
That horror turns into a fright, that turns into tears,
Bleeding on the head, bleeding on the leg,
No one is not scared of the clowns,
They haunt me there, here they shout me, I scream,
I look, they scare, why do clowns go into a closet?
When you are near they take you,
That is a fear of clowns.

Noah Houghton (9)
Button Lane Primary School, Wythenshawe

My Nightmares

If you have a nightmare,
Be prepared for the fright,
It will give you tonight,
Nightmares last for what seems like forever,
But they never,
Unless you don't awake,
It will be stuck in your head,
So you will be filled with dread,
But don't be scared,
It won't be stuck in your bed,
Just in your head.

Lily Lupton (9)
Button Lane Primary School, Wythenshawe

Haunted House

My dog Bruno and my mum left the house. I got so scared that I ran off and got lost. I found a bed and the mattress was as soft as cotton candy. The pillow was as soft as marshmallows. The next morning I saw the exit, but I had to find the key. Suddenly, a clown appeared and chased me. I saw the key on a shelf, grabbed it, opened the door, and ran out.

Ethan Gowrie (9)
Button Lane Primary School, Wythenshawe

The Monster At The End Of My Corridor

One night something as mysterious as a crime scene happened. It started at my sleepover with my friend Archie. When I went to the toilet at exactly 3am I saw an old green monster with a wrinkly face like an old man. I ran up to my bedroom, the light was on shining like a beacon. At that moment I woke up and everything was back to normal.

Kobie Enthwistle (9)
Button Lane Primary School, Wythenshawe

My Pet Rock

My pet rock,
Likes to wear socks,
And likes to read a lot,
We went on a walk,
So he could talk,
Play around until 5 o'clock,
When we got home,
He found my phone,
And saw I had ordered socks,
Now that's the lot,
Now he wears socks,
And that's the story of my pet rock.

Cael Flanagan (9)
Button Lane Primary School, Wythenshawe

Once Upon A Dream

Last night, I had a dream,
A happy dream about my house.
Walls made of marshmallows
A roof of sweets and liquorice

The sky was full of rainbows
Flowers you could not eat
I ate as much as I could
And drank the fizzy Coke
My teeth were still perfect.

Well, until I woke.

River Chipchase (8)
Button Lane Primary School, Wythenshawe

Dreams About Football

Once upon a time, there were two good footballers.
They could jump so high that they could touch the cloudy sky.
But when they landed there was a big boom.
They went onto a big football pitch
That was made of blue bright candyfloss.

Archie Cairns (9)
Button Lane Primary School, Wythenshawe

The Little Boy Who Got Bullied

Once upon a time, there was a little boy who was excited to go to reception for the first time. His mum brought him to the reception on his first day. A couple of days later he was bullied. Some kids were making fun of him, calling him fat and poor.

The kid asked them, "How do you know I'm poor, no one knows that?"

They said, "We just know because of the state of your clothes."

The poor kid said, "Oh."

A few years later he lost his mum and dad, The kids kept bullying him even more and the poor boy started crying every day after school. The kids felt bad for him, so they decided to apologise to him the next day.

The following day they did exactly that and the boy became famous because of what happened to him.

The kids said, "Please can we start all over again? We are so sorry that we bullied you all these years but we felt bad for you, that's why we are asking you now can we be friends?"

He said, "Of course." Then they grew up together as close friends.

Adam Ahmadi (9)

Ecton Brook Primary School, Northampton

The Baby Ballerina

Prance and dance, baby ballerina, all around town,
In the middle of the night, wearing your little crown,
Swirl and twirl, baby ballerina, underneath the stars,
Under the light of the moon and by the fairies, not so far.
Move and groove, baby ballerina, it's your time to shine,
Watch over the fairies all around you as they spread their wings and fly.
Try and fly, little ballerina, let the world see your talent,
Dancing round the streets at night should be a job, not a habit.
Turn and turn, baby ballerina, with your enchanting eyes, shine a blue so bright,
When we look at the stars, all I see is the wonderful light.
Baby ballerina, please help me,
Open my eyes, and let me see.
Baby ballerina, please stop time and let me admire the world you call nice,
Baby ballerina, I guess this is the end,
Send me a postcard to tell me when we will meet again.

Nifermi Kujore (9)
Ecton Brook Primary School, Northampton

The Dream

In my spooky castle, there was a scary and nervous dragon.
Everyone thought the dragon was mean but really the dragon was nice.
I promise you, it was a good dragon.
I went to a cave and he was worried why people were there.
The dragon was lonely.
He didn't have any friends to play with at his school and was bullied for being nice.
No one was nice in his land.
No one was nice to anyone or him.
The cave had a pink room with encrusted diamonds.
I felt serious because everywhere was dark.
I asked the dragon, "Hey, why is everyone's house gloomy in the world?"
The dragon was anxious that everyone would make fun of him because he had a pink room.
He said, "Everyone chased after me!"
They asked, "Can we be friends?"

Lara Hawkins (8)
Ecton Brook Primary School, Northampton

I'm Possible

I have a dream,
I think it is impossible.
I stare into the sky and remember
When I was a little girl, I could see myself on the dancefloor,
I must have been three or four.

I dance until the building shakes,
The crowds would cheer,
The brightness of the spotlight only on me.
The ice-cold dancefloor on my feet
And the music in my ears would not stop.
Because I'm possible.

When the beat gets faster
As my confidence grows like a beanstalk,
I close my eyes,
I can see my future growing and growing
More than I think is possible.

I climb and climb until my dreams come true
And I've reached the top of the world.
All because anything
Is possible.

Isla Edwards (9)
Ecton Brook Primary School, Northampton

Fireflies Alight

In a cold, dark realm I crouch and shiver,
But to my surprise, I see a shimmer.
The flapping of the wings,
The buzzing of the flies,
From a pale flicker,
To immensely lighter.
Curious, I went to investigate,
Hoping to see my mother with a lantern alight.
My emotions switched from cheery to anxious,
As I saw it was only a few flies.
It was different,
With a golden body that sparkled,
Like a fireplace well-lit.
It shone brightly in the moonlit night,
And sent off rays in every direction.
Here and there they glistened in motion,
Under the moonlight like pure gold.
The fireflies smiled in the cold...

Ekene Njoku (8)
Ecton Brook Primary School, Northampton

The Dramatic Performance

B elle glides onto the stage with a smile of joy.

A graceful pirouette and a pretty turn

L eaves the audience wanting more.

L eaping into the air without a care and a twirl en pointe

E agerly, I wait in the wings for my moment to shine.

R ight at the end of her solo, Belle trips and stumbles to the floor

I quickly run on to help her up and guide her off the stage.

N ot wanting to disappoint the audience, I glide on with a smile

A few chaînés and a few petit jetés make them glad

S uddenly, the audience rises and fills the theatre with applause!

Anna Boden (9)

Ecton Brook Primary School, Northampton

A Summer's Day

Every time I go outside,
I have fun on a ride,
Every day the day is hot,
I have ice cream on the spot.

Also, when I get my favourite ice lolly,
I meet this girl called Molly,
At the time I go in,
I have something to put in the bin.

Every time I look at the sky,
I always think I'm going to fly,
At the time I do sports,
After that, I build a fort.

When I have birthday money,
I always have a reason to buy honey,
When I've drawn on a frame,
I always know it doesn't look lame.

Emilia Liutkute (8)
Ecton Brook Primary School, Northampton

The Whale That I Love

He's big and wide,
He loves to splash, he loves to dance,
The day has gone, the days have passed,
He wants to say goodbye with a little splash.

He's as wide as a gate,
He's the colour of a rainbow,
He loves to swim, he loves to play.

The days have passed,
So he swims slower,
The ocean is blue, like him,
So he got taller.

We always stay positive, no matter what,
We always stay kind to people,
We always help as well,
It is very suitable for me to go to the ocean.

Ilinca Tomuz (8)
Ecton Brook Primary School, Northampton

Follow Your Dreams

Follow your dreams high or low
Follow your dreams wherever you go
Follow your dreams big or small
Follow your dreams near or far
Follow your dreams in all directions
Follow your dreams slow or fast
Follow your dreams making memories
Follow your dreams making friends
Follow your dreams inside or outside
Follow your dreams weird or wonderful
Follow your dreams even if it's scary
Follow your dreams even if they change
Follow your dreams, an adventure awaits
Follow your dreams and keep on dreaming.

Elizabeth Marsh (8)
Ecton Brook Primary School, Northampton

My Unicorn

I looked at the sun
A shining ball of light
I got on my unicorn
We flew up high
We went above the clouds
Where it was out of bounds
I looked from above
An amazing sight to see
Evergreen trees
Awaiting for me
I got off her back
And wandered some more
There I stood
At the front door
My unicorn beside me
We took a sneak peek
There inside were many sweets
We began to sit down on the floor
There my unicorn laid
Her tummy grew more.

Sophie Sam (7)
Ecton Brook Primary School, Northampton

Mythology Land

In the real world, I was the best in my class, but I still was filled with rage. So I went to my peaceful place, Mythologyland. There, I saw Thor and Freya, his wife. At the perfect moment, Iron Man came in, glowing like the sun, like the hero he is. Suddenly, the Monkey King came over, so I flew on his mythical cloud and he took me to Zeus Land also called Olympus. When we were there they had a stare-showdown. I laughed. Then I left Mythologyland, went to my bedroom, and went to sleep, dreaming peacefully.

Sam Ojo (9)
Ecton Brook Primary School, Northampton

Mary The Fairy And Mike The Knight

Once upon a dream,
There was a fairy,
Her name was Mary.
She loved berries
And all sorts of sweet fairy magic.
She lived in a beautiful rainbow land called Fairy
And she ate a lot of dairy.
Mary has a dog and she is very hairy
And when she barks she is very scary.
Fairy the land has pink, fluffy clouds that are
marshmallow-like.
When Mary is bored she goes out on her bike,
And her boyfriend is called Mike.
He is a knight
And he likes Nike.

Crystal Whitney (9)
Ecton Brook Primary School, Northampton

My Magical World

A unicorn whisks me away
To a land far away
It's the world of my dreams
There are lush lollipop trees
Sweet candyfloss leaves
I'm as happy as the sunshine
I'm jumping for joy
Just like an overjoyed bunny
But much too soon, you fly me away
I look back, I just want to stay
Then I find I'm back at home all alone
Only a trace of magic in the air
For now, farewell my magical friend.

Amelia-Isabella Child (9)
Ecton Brook Primary School, Northampton

Summer Dream

I'm standing outside of school
And it looks very sunny
I don't have a summer dress on
I only have shorts and a shirt on
I don't care because I am dripping down sweat
I jump, jump and jump until all the sweat comes down
I hide in the trees, the teacher might see me
I won't go outside with my books sneaking
It will be such a shame if someone sees me because I
am sweating.

Moskaa Akbar (7)
Ecton Brook Primary School, Northampton

As Light As A Feather!

If I had wings,
I would fly above the sky.
It would be so easy,
I would barely have to try.
In blue skies and sunny weather,
I'd float along as light as a feather.
I would see a snowflake sparkly and bright,
I'd reach out and touch it, so wispy and light.
As I float down to Earth skies change from dark blue to pink and red.
It's just past 08:00 and I wake in my bed.

Eva Hunt (8)
Ecton Brook Primary School, Northampton

Cricket Trophy

In my dream one night,
I play cricket for Pakistan,
I am the captain of the Pakistani team,
Bright blue sky, sun shining on the ground,
Bronze, silver and gold trophies shining like stars,
Fans cheering for our team,
I can see minty green grass,
I can see green shirts,
My team bang the wickets,
My team is excited, proud and over the moon,
I can see a trophy in my hands.

Muhammad Abubukar Wajid (8)
Ecton Brook Primary School, Northampton

Friendship

It's amazing when people make friends around the world
'Cause when you do, that makes God laugh and twirl.
So do try and make friends even though you fall apart, just fix it and then you are happy.
Oh, and did I tell you that some friends are *really chatty!*
No one gets hurt if everyone plays nicely.
So do make sure that you say your statements precisely.

Smaranda Juravschi (8)
Ecton Brook Primary School, Northampton

Love

Some people are infatuated
Sometimes love is inherited.
Some love has ascended
Lovers are soft-headed
And that is quite impressive.
But when it is old, it grows cold.
Give me a boat that will
Carry two and both shall row
My love and I.
If this love ceases to exist
I shall not cry.
And I shall watch the
Love flow by.

Yasmin Broomes (8)
Ecton Brook Primary School, Northampton

Little Star

Little star, you shine so bright,
When I lay my head in the night,
When I close my eyes, I see you shine,
Then I wish you were mine.
Going round you, I see fairies going by,
As they fly and fly,
Now I open my eyes, the sun is bright,
Now I know, I have the might,
So I will see you again tonight.

Fifimay Wall (9)
Ecton Brook Primary School, Northampton

Untitled

I like to dance in the rain,
I love to dance in the snow
But most of all,
I like dancing on my own.
It makes me feel happy
It makes me feel calm
When I dance, it makes the time pass.
Wherever I do it at home
Or in class
No matter where or when
I feel complete at last.

Lenae Kennedy (8)
Ecton Brook Primary School, Northampton

My Dream To See The People Who Died In The Past

My Aunt Tracey died when I was six, nearly seven. I really miss her. She always used to cheer me up. I felt sad. My nan Pauline died when I was four, I really miss her. She was so kind. My nan's cat Timmy, I used to play with him all the time. They are shining stars in the night. I look up to them, I miss them.

Ruben Sanders (9)
Ecton Brook Primary School, Northampton

Seeds To Sow

Once I wanted a seed to sow
So a beautiful plant will grow
I put soil in a pot
The seed I selected was a dicot
Sunlight, right temperature and a water shower
I provided it all to bloom my flower.

Maryam Naseem (8)
Ecton Brook Primary School, Northampton

Lost In A Dream

L ost in a dream, no way to get out

O utside you and your friends are playing.

S uddenly your dream changes and, "Wow!" you say

T ime has changed and I'm with the Saxons...

I nside it feels like a dream bubble, you can't imagine

N ow I'm building the pyramids with the Egyptians...

A nimals are humongous in the dream.

D inosaurs, unicorns, dragons and mythical creatures

R eading books helps my brain grow

E ntering Narnia, seeing Mr Tumnus and having tea

A nd taking on a gladiator, winning a medal

M y dream has ended and I'm just lying in bed.

Anna Thompson (9)
Hart Plain Junior School, Waterlooville

Mystery Of The Sky

Up, up into the sky,
Something is there,
I don't know why.

It could be a threat,
That I need to fight.
Or, it could be something,
Of pure delight.

How will I find it?
What will I do?
Transport a spaceship
To give me a clue.

I am an astronaut,
As smart as can be.
I just can't wait to be up there,
And see what's in front of me.

Sooner or later,
I will find out.
The mystery will be revealed
Without a doubt!

Oliver James (9)
Hart Plain Junior School, Waterlooville

Whispers Of Fairyland

In forests green where moonlight gleams,
Fairies dance and share their dreams.
With wings so bright, they soar and play,
Making my magic every day.

So close your eyes and make a wish,
For fairies grant them with a swish.
In tales of wonder, they'll always stay,
Bringing magic your 9-year-old way.

In meadows green where dreams take flight,
Fairies dance in the soft moonlight.
With twinkling eyes and laughter bring,
They paint the stars in the velvet night.

Sofia Gisby (9)
Hart Plain Junior School, Waterlooville

Nightmare

N ightmares are scary
I magine getting chased by clowns
G etting lost in a fantasy world
H unted by animals which can kill you
T he mysterious rainfall
M ajestically shining
A ttacked by a serial killer
R unning fast for your life, noticing
E verything is a dream.

Flora Haastrup (8)
Hart Plain Junior School, Waterlooville

Clowns

C ruel weird monster-type creatures

L urking under my bed in the night

O nly me in my bed, feeling terrified

W aiting, anticipating for the morning to come

N ow I know it is not long before sunrise

S unlight finally awakens me, I realise it is only a
dream.

Scarlett-Rose Downer (8)

Hart Plain Junior School, Waterlooville

Good Night, Sleep Tight

Good night, sleep tight
Once you are asleep you are very light,
In your mind, there could be a bee,
Or your name could be Lee or Phoebe,
It's up to you,
Do what you want to do,
Good night,
Sleep tight,
Sweet dreams.

Phoebe Kramer (9)
Hart Plain Junior School, Waterlooville

Magical Universe

M ust you close eyes and dream, dream where your imagination takes you,

A mazing dreams take you to space, where aliens are, and that's the one where this is placed,

G lancing left and right in a rocket far from Earth,

I magination is something big,

C an imagination get too big? No, it can't.

A world far bigger than Earth, the Dream World.

L ack of intelligence, aliens attacking the Dream World,

U nlimited dreams happening at the same time as being attacked,

N othing can stop them, unless...

I f we stop them using a poem, this one!

V ortex the poem to the aliens,

E liminate the aliens using the poem,

R esting in bed,

S un rises up,

E nough for tonight, got to use the energy.

Usman Samaiga (8)
Lea Forest Primary Academy, Kitts Green

Nara's Dream

Once, there was a little boy called Nara.
Nara's dream was to go to space,
But sadly it was a dream he never faced.
Day after day he hoped it would come true,
But then, one day, a letter came through.

Finally, this was it, he could finally live his dream!
But he wasn't quite ready and was not full of ease.
Well, this wasn't easy for Nara - he had a home,
He didn't want to leave his sweet, beautiful home.

The day had come and his heart was racing,
But he'd dreamt of it for years, so he should just face it.
He got on the rocket with butterflies in his stomach.
When they got into space, they could see the stars in
the distance.
As they got closer, they saw lots of planets,
But Nara was still in a panic.

The first stop was to the moon, as the rocket landed,
he dropped.
One step he took, Nara wasn't so worried anymore,
The more he travelled, the more he became fearless.
He was having fun, yet he was on track,
But he got a message saying it was time to go back.

He jumped, he leapt, he climbed and jived,
Yet he was ready to go to his family hive.
"Nara, Nara, please wake up," pleaded his mother,
Then his sister said he was being a bother.
He then woke up in a hurry,
Then said, "I'm back already."

No one knew what he was talking about.
Turns out this was all a dream.

Georgia Payal (8)
Lea Forest Primary Academy, Kitts Green

The Mystical Pillow Palace

What in the world was that all about? Oh, hi there, I'm Khizer! I've just been through an insane experience at the moment. It was a dream about this err... creepy Pillow Palace. I'll tell you all about it! Here we go. After a blink of an eye, I mysteriously appeared in front of this massive palace. I felt lost. Anyways, I was like why don't I discover it? Or should I... Anyways, I took the mortifying risk and galloped in. Oh my goodness. It was full of pillows, blankets, plushies and teddies! Felt quite suspicious, but nobody could resi- *Creak!* The misty moon glared at me as the breezy wind bolted past me. What was that noise all about? What was going on? Was this a bad idea after all? I felt absolutely aghast! Something caught my eye in the distance...

It was like a pillow monster with eyes that sparkled like diamonds, surrounded by soft pink pillows and blankets as fluffy as clouds. Its face looked as mortifying as a tarantula coming to seek your warm, juicy blood! It chased me as I squealed with terror running down my head to my tips. As I hid under the blanket... Clutch! It was too late, it had caught me... Before it got a chance to gobble me up. *Gasp!* I found myself sitting up on my bed at 6am in the morning, wondering what it was, to the realisation it was all a dream and there was no Pillow Palace or pillow monsters... or are there?

Khizer Ali (10)
Lea Forest Primary Academy, Kitts Green

Almost My Dream Land

Once upon a dream, I was in a forest but it wasn't an ordinary forest. It was a forest filled with sweets! There were flakes instead of trees and gummy pencils for vines and the ground was made out of chocolate. I couldn't believe my eyes. I wondered if I was dreaming. *What is happening? I think I just need a drink...* but, *wait!* The river was made of chocolate milk! As I took a sip, I saw it. It was a monster. It had candyfloss for hair. I really couldn't bear it!

I ran as fast as I could but he did too. It was too late, I had to accept my fate. *Crash! Bang!* Suddenly my rescue arrived, and I realised I could chill and thrive. As I left the island I looked up at the sky and waved goodbye. As I woke up I started to blink and think, *was it all just a dream? Or was it not...?*

Maria Bibi (10)
Lea Forest Primary Academy, Kitts Green

A Dream Dollshouse

A dventure will come

D awn by day

R ainbow and kittens

E very step I take it gets more creepy like clowns

A dream dollhouse they say! No way!

M aybe it could, or rather not hey?

D elusional dollhouse more like!

O r maybe not... this is just chaos!

L ove is all we need! Oh and lots of glitter.

L ike it doesn't sound too bad now.

H elp is something we do not need!

O f course not, it's beautiful

U nderestimate our power. Maybe we should do this after

S illy, of course not, I'm never doing this again.

E ver so what if it's a dream?

I open my eyes... Poof, it's all gone!

Imarah Uddin (7)
Lea Forest Primary Academy, Kitts Green

Magical Dollhouse!

In this poem, magical dolls are revealed!
Rainbows and fairies,
A magical world!
But don't forget there's a bad side too!
I've been told there's a magical dollhouse somewhere!
No, it can't be so,
There's a magical dollhouse somewhere, here!
And it's not a lie!
Lena and Lisa were somewhere there!
Oh my gosh! It can't be true!
But it is!
And in that dollhouse, there's all sorts...
There are cotton candy clouds as sweet as can be.
Beautiful, beautiful, beautiful!
I love the magical dollhouse world!
It's amazing! It's mind-numbing!
And it's totally true!
If you want to come, just close your eyes!
And into a world of such surprise...
See you there!

Zara Alam (8)
Lea Forest Primary Academy, Kitts Green

Magical World

M y dream world starts with a little girl.

A beautiful little girl with sparkly yellow hair.

G radually, she walks to a portal and she went in...

I n a flash, she appears in a magical world...

C overed in bubblegum, the sun began to explode.

A nimals licking the chocolate floors as well as doors.

L una couldn't help but do it too!

W *ow!* she thought...

"O h my god!" she said out loud as she saw the horses.

R ight in front of her, the fairy's wings sparkled.

L oving this world, she had to leave.

D reams are imagination...

Tamsin Dumitrascu (7)

Lea Forest Primary Academy, Kitts Green

My Mythical Adventure

Once there was a boy
That had tons of joy.
One day there was a lion, a flying one!
He said, "Hop on my back,"
I thought I would call him Captain Underpants or
SpongeBob.
We ended up in a forest,
But a magical mythical forest.
I saw a flying horse
That shook its butt, it was happy.
Then I saw something I couldn't unsee,
A lava *dragon!*
Then incredibly, I thought it was cool and hot,
It was a half-crystal, half-fire.
Then it was time to go home,
I hopped on Captain Underpants or SpongeBob,
Because he was a lion.
I thought he would put my leg
In a peg
And eat it!

Kayden Coates (9)
Lea Forest Primary Academy, Kitts Green

Free Palestine

Free Palestine, we cry out loud,
For justice, for peace and freedom proud.
A land of beauty, history and pain,
We long to see it thrive again.

The olive trees, the sunsets bright,
The Gaza Strip, a constant fight for basic rights.
For dignity, for children to play,
And be carefree.

From the river to the sea,
Palestine will one day be free.
No walls, no checkpoints,
No fear, just love, unity and cheer.

So raise your voice and stand with pride,
For Palestine, our hearts abide.
Let's work together hand in hand,
To free this, free this precious, sacred land.

Mariam Iqbal Ali (9)
Lea Forest Primary Academy, Kitts Green

Dreams

In my dreams every night,
The enchanted forest was a beautiful sight,
My friends and I see fairies fly,
To my amazement, I join them in the sky,
I fall back down to the ground,
And enter a room with zero sound,
I see an array of sweets around,
"Wow," I gasp, as I realise what I've found,
My tummy starts to rumble so I eat a handful of sweets,
I can't believe my dream is in a land of treats,
I made the most of the time I have here,
The morning light is near,
What a blast I've had in the secret room,
I hope to come back here soon.

Aizah Waqas (8)
Lea Forest Primary Academy, Kitts Green

The Sweet Fairy Forest

I once dreamed about a sweet fairy forest,
Sweet cotton candy clouds,
Gummy flowers, blueberry frosting for the sky,
Gingerbread houses and people,
A Coke river,
Am I dreaming? I thought to myself,
I felt happy and delighted,
I had my friend right by my side.

D ream big
R eally dream
E ntertain your dream
A n amazing dream
M aintain and enjoy your dream.

All I could see was gingerbread people with sour belts for hair and clothes, it was weird but really fun and entertaining. This was not the end.

Esme Matthews (10)
Lea Forest Primary Academy, Kitts Green

Candy World

Candy, candy, candy world,
I'm dreaming of a candy world.
Cotton candy trees
With sugar-stealing bees,
Rivers full of gems and jellies.
My eyes are bigger than my belly.
Lollipops growing in the grass,
I'm gobbling them up so fast.
Mountains made of toffee,
They look kind of sloppy.
My tummy's filling up quickly,
I'm feeling quite sickly.
Now it's time to leave this yummy land of treats
And see what my mum has made to eat.
I can't wait to see
Where I'll go
The next time
I fall asleep.

Khadijah Love (10)
Lea Forest Primary Academy, Kitts Green

Wonder Ruby Funland

In my dreams every night,
I rise up into the sky so bright,
My friend so near to tears,
I help her conquer all her fears,
Bumper cars bumping,
Children jumping,
Lights flashing,
Children dashing,
All around me are crazy clowns,
And children in dressing gowns,
I have no idea what's going on,
It's really time to get gone!
My friends disappear and so do the clowns,
The world goes silent with absolutely no sounds,
Time to sleep soundly is finally here,
But light shines through my curtain... the morning is near!

Zahra Balić (7)
Lea Forest Primary Academy, Kitts Green

Magical World

M ost magical place you've ever been to
A ll the creatures you'd ever imagine greet you
G igantic animals and small mammals
I n the most magical place you've ever been to
C ome, come, you'll have the best time of your life!
A dventure this island if you dare
L ove adventuring, this is the place for you

W ould you come?
O ver the Milky Way you'll find us
R eady when you are
L et's go!
D ream, dream, dream, enjoy your stay!

Charlie Stretton-Yeomans (8)
Lea Forest Primary Academy, Kitts Green

Monster Land

M iles away from where we live but on the same planet

O ther things rule

N ow they're trying to take over the world

S o guess what they're called

T hey're monsters of course!

E rrrr, if you never knew, all of them go

R *oar, roar, roar!*

L ots of them have huge menacing claws

A nd

N ow we need to protect the human race

D o you want to join us? If you do close, your eyes and we'll see you on the other side.

Neo Montaque (8)

Lea Forest Primary Academy, Kitts Green

Dream Royal

In my dreams every night,
I sleep so, so tight.
My thoughts drift off to a royal time,
In hope the kingdom will become mine.
I see the sky too, look how bright
But when I look back, I don't see so much light.
I find myself in a dark, dark place,
Tears begin to run down my face.
Then a flash, a bang,
A clap.
I fall down a magical trap.
Surrounded by royalty, I feel at home,
I will never ever be alone.
I become the princess of the land
And the handsome prince takes my hand.

Amelia Caines (8)
Lea Forest Primary Academy, Kitts Green

My Dragon

That's my dragon!
Swooping up, ever so high,
Frightening people below,
I'm not scared, are you?
Fire breather,
Noise maker,
Ear acher,
Fear maker,
Bone breaker,
High flyer,
Low swooper,
Dentist hater.

D rags its prey home,
R uining buildings in its way,
A ngry noises echoing around,
G round shakes, announcing its arrival,
O range fire blazes out of its nostrils,
N ot a good night when dragons are around.

Haniya Abbas (9)
Lea Forest Primary Academy, Kitts Green

Sea Monster!

In my dreams every night,
I dive down deep into the ocean bright.
A shadow appears,
I really want it to disappear.
It tangles me up with its tentacles long,
Will I ever escape... it is so *strong!*
It pulls and pulls so tight,
It gives me such a fright.
I realise I have a pin,
And I poke it in its skin.
It deflates in a flash,
So I quickly make a dash.
Now I'm safe back in bed,
So I can finally rest my head.

Dominic Flynn (8)
Lea Forest Primary Academy, Kitts Green

Side By Side

Blood-gurgling scream,
Tiny whiny children run and hide
And fall down the ghost slide,
Running and running until I saw the other side.
Life is like a dream,
That is a mystery, as it may seem.
Pink fog cleared in a blink.
Purple birds tweeted,
As the smell of sweet, delicious sweets
Filled the air.
Rainbow, swirling, twirling lollipops
Dancing like it was floating on air.
I then *awoke...*

Anaya Arshad (10)
Lea Forest Primary Academy, Kitts Green

Dinosaur Planet

In my dreams every night,
Dinosaurs may bite,
Armed with swords and shields held tight,
My friends and I are ready to fight,
Surprisingly the dinosaurs fight each other,
So we just watch and take cover,
The dinosaurs tire and start to fall asleep,
We come out of our hiding spot to have a little peep,
It's time to escape and go back to my bed,
That is the perfect place to rest my head.

George McLaughlin (8)
Lea Forest Primary Academy, Kitts Green

A Little Girl...

A little girl
Who flies to the sun,
She really loves the hairstyle
The bun.
She flies to space
At a steady pace.
In a mysterious room
A witch was riding on a broom.
Flying to a star,
with a very bright mark.
She's on the moon
Exactly at noon.
At last, she looks up to the sky
And waves goodbye.

Inshrah Butt (9)
Lea Forest Primary Academy, Kitts Green

The Candy Land

I was by myself
And I was just walking and
Days and days went past
And everything changed
The Candy Land was amazing
All the houses and shops turned into sweets and
All of the trees turned into lollipops
The flowers turned into sweets.
The grass was hard
Chocolate when you walk.
It was just amazing, I loved it!

Maisie Tighe (9)
Lea Forest Primary Academy, Kitts Green

Magical World

Excited faces dance,
Sparkly unicorns floating around like balloons,
A fountain full of melted chocolate,
Faces splashed with sparkly colours,
If you want to visit, just close your eyes.

Alina Barak (8)
Lea Forest Primary Academy, Kitts Green

Lots Of Mess

Daring
Ride
Everlasting
Make it the best
When I woke up I was in a castle and the room was a mess,
I looked up and there was a loose flower on the desk,
I did not know what to do next.
There was a person cleaning up,
Just when I was going to lean back,
When my back started to crack.
The person said to go outside,
So I did and there was a slide,
A person came out and lied.
They said it was boring!
The castle was made out of chocolate,
I thought it was a dream
Until I saw a green tea and a team
But they were mean
So I got some green tea,
But I found myself in a tree,
A pegasus came along, so I went on,
I fell off in the air,

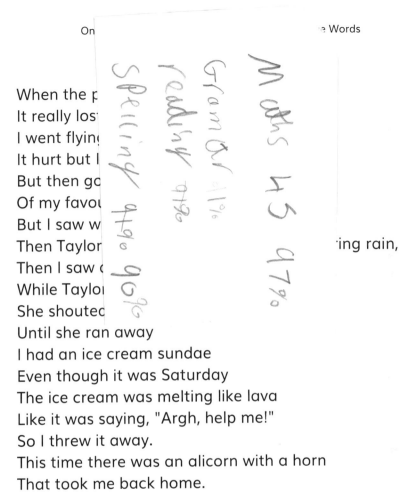

When the p

It really los

I went flying

It hurt but I

But then go

Of my favou

But I saw w

Then Taylor　　　　　　　　　　　　　　ing rain,

Then I saw

While Taylo

She shoutec

Until she ran away

I had an ice cream sundae

Even though it was Saturday

The ice cream was melting like lava

Like it was saying, "Argh, help me!"

So I threw it away.

This time there was an alicorn with a horn

That took me back home.

Mara O'Sullivan Candela (9)

Staynor Hall Community Primary Academy, Selby

The Unicorn Story

Once there was a unicorn. It lived in a village up in the clouds.

But this unicorn was astonishing. It was so amazing you can't possibly imagine it.

There weren't just lots of unicorns, there was also a girl called Maddie.

She was the master of the village.

There was one playground, three swimming pools and ten fast-food shops like KFC.

Every year the village got bigger and bigger!

The next day they saw a new path

So everyone went up and saw a huge castle

They opened the door and a girl was standing there

She greeted them and she said, "Hi, my name is Leela."

The master said, "I am Maddie."

Leela said, "Come, I will show you around."

After that, Maddie said, "Do you want to come to my home?"

Leela said, "Yes," so she did.

At the village they camped in a forest next to a playground.

They played in the playground and then they went into a tent.

They sang spooky stories and then they went to sleep in the forest but they could not.
Maddie said, "Why don't we have a KFC."
Then they all went to sleep.

Madelyn Simpson (7)

Staynor Hall Community Primary Academy, Selby

My Dream

The dancer is reading a wand on the dancefloor in the middle of the night.
The child is clapping in the crowd on the roof before the show.
The ringmaster is shouting at performers in the night sky in the morning.
The king is waving to the stars in the distance during the interval.
Batman is hiding from the performers on the roof in the middle of the night.
The acrobats are dancing in the stars outside the tent after the applause.
The dragon is eating a book in the spotlight during the interval.
Spider-Man is dancing with a map in his pocket on his day off.
The writer is cheering in the spotlight behind a chair, later on.
The T-rex is reading to the crowd on a chair in summer.
The king is eating on a bench in the doorway on Friday.
Batman is throwing air into the night sky in his spare time.
The T-rex is eating popcorn on the dancefloor after the applause.

The dancer is swimming on the roof in the summer.
Superman is having a bath in the evening.
I am flying with a wand in the countryside on Friday.

Jordan Banton (7)
Staynor Hall Community Primary Academy, Selby

My Dog Ivy And I

Once upon a time, there was a dog in the fog,
Who was eating a slimy, gross frog.
Then, a girl came along and twirled,
Her name was Pearl.
Pearl found the dog and took it home.

On the way the dog sat on a log,
They eventually were at the house,
And found a mouse!
She makes the dog her pet,
Gets it to the vets,
Because it had lots of scratches,
Which makes her upset.

He hid in a basket,
But a handbasket.
The dog crawled to a ball and
Bounced on the wall.
The wall was very tall,
The vet was called Paul.
He was so scared, he hurried to go in,
But he was prepared.

He had big patches of scratches.
The vet put lots of plaster on because
He was a master.
The next day,
I went with my dog and the headmaster said,
"That's cute."
Pearl said, "Thank you very much."

The next day, Pearl named the dog Ivy.
They both loved mac and cheese,
So they shoved it in their mouths.

Abigail Graham (8)

Staynor Hall Community Primary Academy, Selby

Miss Sparks' Magical Home

Miss Sparks' magical home is in the sky with no lights, floating in the air. She had moonlight in her hair. Then I went to Miss Sparks' house and I said, "Wow! Look at you! You are a very beautiful lady, why?"

Miss Sparks said, "Because I'm going out to vote to be the president of the United States."

Then we went home and found a treasure chest and it had some paper in it that said, *If you keep praying, you will be the president.*

Day after day she kept on praying and putting out her name in the vote. But day after day she lost to Donald Trump.

Then one day she said, "This is my last day voting," so she went to put her name in, but there were already a lot of people there so that meant she had a really big challenge.

She went home, listened to the radio and then she still didn't make it. So, she went to the shop, got some sweets and watched a good story in her bedroom. She was crying, and so upset.

Esme Cleary (7)
Staynor Hall Community Primary Academy, Selby

Kitty And The Magical Land

Once there was a cat called Kitty. She was very pretty and very cute, better than the sound 'toot'.

When Kitty sleeps, she's very dreamy, and when she dreams, her head is filled with happiness, and she sleeps soundly in her bed.

She hates going to the vet but she does like getting wet. She's very cute. She's very pretty, but most of all, she loves adventure. Yes, she loves adventure!

One day, she had an amazing adventure because she'd wished upon a star and her wishes came true, and when she told her adopted sister Poppy the alien about it, she was excited as well!

They both went to a magical land and it was just like her dream. There were cupcakes, clouds and gingerbread houses, and there was more candy, but most of all, there was a unicorn panda and a unicorn. The unicorn panda was just like in her dream!

Maya Ritchie (8)
Staynor Hall Community Primary Academy, Selby

My Future Dream

A n amazing feeling,
C hasing my dream,
T he place, the time,
O rdinary people in my life
R iding and living the dream.

I'm on stage, can't you see?
I'm as excited as I can be!
The audience is filled with people, including my close
friends,
We are doing the latest trends.
I'm going on stage,
Don't worry, I've been paid my wage!
I'm in a movie and
It's time to get groovy.
I'm dancing right now, I can't believe that's my dream,
Wow! I'm about to scream,
I've finished the movie,
I swear one of the boys went to juvie,
I'm watching it now and I can see myself,
This is the end, thank you for listening,
I'm sure your dream will come true if it is glistening.

Harper Jackson (9)
Staynor Hall Community Primary Academy, Selby

The Midnight Sky

Every time I look through my window at night, I don't like to look at the birds or bats, I look at the cats, and the sky.

I see black cats painting the sky purple, green and blue. One time I turned into a giant black cat, and every time I laid my black paw on the sky, the sky changed colour. I heard the other black cats *meowing* in the dead of night, and all the black cats were snuggled up in the blanket of midnight.

And then I snuggled up to the others and I finally fell asleep.

When I woke up I was back into a human again. *How weird*, I thought, *it must have been a dream.*

But it was actually real, and when I looked through the window, I didn't see any black cats anymore.

Instead, I saw giant golden dogs painting the morning sky blue.

Áine Ritchie (8)
Staynor Hall Community Primary Academy, Selby

Knock, Knock, Knock

Tip, tap, tip, tap was the echoing sound,
That was the only sound around.
Dragons flew over my head.
They were really filling me with dread.

The bees danced.
The stars pranced.
Still, the only sound,
Was the tip-tap all around.

I've reached a cottage that was as black as a black
hole,
Then I saw a carriage standing next to a pole.

I knocked on the door of the cottage.
Knock, knock, knock.
Ding, dong, ding, dong chimed the clock.

There was no answer, so I knocked again.
Knock. Knock. Knock. It started to rain,
So I turned and walked away.
The only sound,
Was the tip-tap echoing all around.

Then someone, or something, stood there on the ground.
Never to be found.

Katelyn Watson-Frank (9)
Staynor Hall Community Primary Academy, Selby

My Bizarre Dream!

D reams too much!
R eads too many fairy tales!
E asily distracted!
A lways ready for a surprise!
M oves from one dream to another!

I'm on the stage,
The audience keeps looking from me to their lyric page,
I sound like Taylor Swift,
But then I smell a familiar whiff,
The lights go off, it is dark,
It's like when I walk home from the park,
First, I can only see a pink cat with fluffy fur,
But, "Oh no," it doesn't purr,
It growls like a tiger and laughs like a clown,
Then I see it wearing its rainbow clown hair, it is a clown...
As a crown!
I run as fast as I can!
I'm safe for now,
From the creepy clown!

Sofia Hammill (9)
Staynor Hall Community Primary Academy, Selby

Back In The Past

Once upon a time, there was a young boy called Leo and his favourite thing was dinosaurs. He played with his toy dinosaurs and wished they were real. One night, Leo wished dinosaurs were alive for one day and fell asleep.

When Leo woke up, he heard a loud... *roar!* Leo opened his window and saw... a *T-rex!* He also saw an apatosaurus eating some tree leaves from his back garden.

Then, Leo went downstairs, ate breakfast and got dressed. Leo went into his garden and saw a stegosaurus. Leo said, "This is the best day ever!"

Ten hours later, it was time for Leo's bed, so Leo went to bed. When Leo woke up, he looked out his window and it was all back to normal!

Leo Chambers (7)
Staynor Hall Community Primary Academy, Selby

The Octopus Nightmare

Once upon a time, there was a wizard,
And he had magical beans.
Bang! The wizard disappeared.
Before he disappeared, he said, "Whoosh!"
Then one day, a magical octopus was hiding under the kids' bed,
And pulled one off.
The kid grabbed the beans and ate them,
And turned into a beast so he could destroy the octopus
And the kid won, all because the magical wizard saved the kid,
And the kid lived happily ever after.
And when the kids grew up, they had kids too
And there was one more bean left,
And one ate it and turned into a beast
And went outside and God saved his life and saved the world.

Reid Reclusado (8)
Staynor Hall Community Primary Academy, Selby

Football Stadium

F ields full of footballs. What are we going to do?

O pen the pitch and let the footballers begin.

O ver the goal into the crowd.

T op of the league.

B alls flying everywhere, dive and catch them whenever.

A ll around blowing footballs swishing in the air.

L aughing, giggling, football is such fun!

L oving friends to play football.

S ometimes louder than it's supposed to be.

T all as a skyscraper.

A lways exciting.

D efinitely, I'm meant to have one.

I s sometimes scary.

U nstoppable.

M astered.

Finlay Lawrence (9)
Staynor Hall Community Primary Academy, Selby

A Nightmare

I took a step somewhere unknown. I'm alone. All there was, was a... bird? This bird didn't chirp though. it growled. It growled louder than a lion! For some reason, it was a rainbow bird. Then I realised it was a clown! One of my fears!

I ran off thinking I was in the clear of my fear. Then a beast hungry for a feast came to me. I realised it had just seen the food behind me!

I sat down, but forgot all about the clown. The clown! The *clown!* How could I forget? Obviously it ran away as soon as it saw the beast. The clown thought it was the beast's feast!

11 years later, me and that beast are besties!

Isabelle Fitch (9)
Staynor Hall Community Primary Academy, Selby

Midnight Dreams

As the day came to an end,
Getting in my car and driving home,
As I make my dinner,
Getting in my pyjamas, all snug and warm,
Jumping into bed was my happy place after all.
Drifting to sleep.
In my dream I saw clouds and black misty skies,
Getting pulled up by the stars.
I stood up and I was walking on clouds.
I was floating.
Waking up, I felt joyful and happy after work.
Having a shower, dinner, and sprinting for my magical
dream,
Flying on space horses.
My little sister woke me up...
And from now I will never forget,
My magical stunning dreams.

Ruby Turnbull (9)
Staynor Hall Community Primary Academy, Selby

Magical Meadow Dream

In this dream, I think about every night,
There is no such thing as fright,
It was like I'm in a fairy tale,
And nothing, just nothing is pale,
Magic lives here, no lie,
So everything here cannot die,
I am in a magic meadow,
Where the warm wind has a gentle blow,
And if I look closely,
I can see fairies,
There, just over by the bushes,
Picking berries,
All of a sudden, the trees start dancing,
The flowers start singing,
And the fairies start prancing,
I've woken up now,
But the dream was... just wow.

Bridget Thornton (8)
Staynor Hall Community Primary Academy, Selby

Once Upon A Dream

Once upon a dream,
In a land far away,
There lived a dancer,
People called her a prancer.
When it rained she did her sad day routine,
When it was sunny, she did her happy day play,
A magical unicorn was her friend,
They were friends till the end.
On stage, she was like a sparkler,
She would never be a burglar,
She made everybody happy,
She even made dogs less snappy.
When she danced,
It was like the crowd's eyes were playing tricks,
The air tasted like buttercream,
So thanks for listening to my dream.

Leela Snowdon (8)
Staynor Hall Community Primary Academy, Selby

Once Upon A Dream

Once upon a dream, I woke up in the desert.
I walked forward to a shocking scene.
I saw my dog sitting in the teacher's chair!
We went on a school trip.
Although we went on a ship,
I still managed to slip.
Once we arrived I caught my dog,
Standing on a log, eating a frog!
"I hate the terrible weather,"
As it started to rain and fog.
After that we came across a slug,
Eating a bug and named him Mob!
Next I came across my dog on a different log,
Falling off into the same frog he ate!

Layla Grace Cleary (9)
Staynor Hall Community Primary Academy, Selby

The Scary Clowns And Aliens

Once, I woke up in a dream,
I heard a scream,
I jumped out of my bed
And saw a horrifying scene.
I saw clowns dancing around,
Suddenly, I heard a weird sound,
The clown threw me into the air,
I found myself sitting in a chair,
The next thing I saw were aliens
Wiggling around,
Then I found
Myself in a terrible position.

The clown's face was as scary as a tarantula,
The alien's face was as funny as a cat in sunglasses,
The clown's red nose was as funny as a chicken.

Poppy Roberts (8)
Staynor Hall Community Primary Academy, Selby

The Unicorn Like Me

I see a teacher teaching in a school,
There is a unicorn, I pet it,
The unicorn is soft, pink and fluffy.
"Unicorn," I say, "I like you."
Pizza is yummy and enjoyable,
I tell the unicorn a joke.
"Why did the man cross the road?"
The unicorn said, "Why?"
I said, "To get to the other side!"
What a great dream!
I hope I have another one of those dreams
I hope I see a unicorn in my dream again,
I love that purple unicorn.

Joshua Bradshaw (8)
Staynor Hall Community Primary Academy, Selby

The Football Dream

Poppy K and I went to the football stadium. All my family came to watch me and twenty minutes later the game started. Someone slide-tackled me, but I slide-tackled them back and then I scored! All my family cheered for me and Poppy cheered for me as well. After half-time, the game started again and Poppy got slide-tackled. Poppy also slide-tackled them back, and then Poppy scored! The game stopped and our team won! Then we were in the finals! Everyone was cheering for our team.

Harrison Boland (9)
Staynor Hall Community Primary Academy, Selby

A Football Match With Dragons

Once upon a time, a football match was on, and a dragon came along and scored a goal. So the score was 1 to Birmingham and 0 to Coventry.

Two more dragons came to the football match, and one of the dragons scored a goal. So the score was 2 to Birmingham and 0 to Coventry.

Birmingham was winning and the third dragon scored a goal, so the score was 3 to Birmingham and 0 to Coventry.

People threw a pie in my house, and I jumped into a swimming pool.

Oliver Lees (8)
Staynor Hall Community Primary Academy, Selby

Flying Pirates

Pirates are dirty, selfish and mean
And they have nothing to care about.
Indeed but these pirates are different.
These pirates can fly and they kidnap people in their
sleep.
When you awaken you will see scary things on the ship.
There is one thing you will never see...
Your loving family again.
But there is one more thing that can happen...
A good, happy, kind, adventurous, big, fluffy, purple
monster will save you!

Oscar Chambers (9)
Staynor Hall Community Primary Academy, Selby

Cat Ball!

C at Ball is an imaginary fun sport and you can eat runaway chocolate!

A lso, you can eat diving popcorn, diving into your mouth.

T hen the match starts.

"B alls coming everywhere, ahhhhh!" screamed a player.

A cat leader says, "Here comes a catnami!"

"L alalalalalaaaaaa!" sang the cat king.

"L a," said a cat leader and... the end!

Philip Arrighi (8)
Staynor Hall Community Primary Academy, Selby

Me And My Magical Dragon

Once upon a dream, there was a dragon in a damp cave. His claws were as sharp as laser-sharp teeth. His wings were as wide as a hippo. When he breathed out fire it was as hot as the sun. In the dream, I got on his back and we flew into space, to see Harry, the Formula One racetrack and the whole Milky Way. We flew around the galaxy. I hope you enjoyed my dream, now I will go and eat some buttercream. Sleep tight, don't let the bed bugs bite!

Noah Seagrave (8)
Staynor Hall Community Primary Academy, Selby

Football In Space

I am heading to the moon
I am getting there soon
I am there now
There is a football pitch, wow!
I have found a ball now
I was about to score
The ball got away from me, there was a dinosaur
We met a dragon
We had to chase the ball
We got the ball
The dragon was tall
The dragon flew away
And landed upside down
The dinosaur was about to score
But it scored on my head, it hurt.

Joshua Terry (9)
Staynor Hall Community Primary Academy, Selby

The Imaginary Dreams

Among you are the dragons,
There are big and small dragons,
Mini dragons run around because they are
mischievous!
But big dragons hide as they like to stay hush.

Unicorn horns are shivering with excitement,
They are tiny, cool unicorns,
Magical unicorns,
Rainbow unicorns,
And beautiful unicorns.

Into these dreams,
You can come too,
But only if you believe they are true!

Marceline Lindley (8)
Staynor Hall Community Primary Academy, Selby

A Magic Meadow

A beautiful meadow filled with trees.
A fantastic smell is weaved into the breeze.
You never know what you will meet.
Pretty porcupines or pretty geese?
Unicorns and fairies in the sky.
One thing I can tell you is that they never lie.
The happiest creatures I'll ever meet.
The amazing meadow beneath my feet.
Wanting to stay and play all day,
I have to wake up, there is school today.

Jessica Chambers (8)
Staynor Hall Community Primary Academy, Selby

My Dream

I can see the meadow with the hills and a rabbit passing by with a fuzzy tail. I look up at the sky and I can see the stars. I look up at the moon shining bright in the sky. I look at the rabbit slurping up water. It sounds like a tap dripping. I go to stroke the rabbit but it runs fast like fire. I see something in the bushes, so I go towards it and it is a unicorn. It is pink and white, beautiful and amazing. It even has wings.

Vienna Burgos-Crossley (8)
Staynor Hall Community Primary Academy, Selby

Once Upon A Circus

I skipped to the circus one night,
And I got a terrific fright,
It was quiet in the circus,
All of a sudden
A clown appeared from the shadows,
His nose was like a fire bolt,
I ran out the circus
Like a rat dashing,
I ran to the forest
And the trees got nearer.
I sprinted to my mum and dad's room,
Now I am safe in there.
I've never had another dream like that again!

Theo Bailey (8)
Staynor Hall Community Primary Academy, Selby

Oh, Chaos In The Sky

Oh no! There is chaos in the sky,
Up so high, oh why?
Why are we up so high? thought I
They are faster than a racing car
Argh! A dragon is having a dragon party in my wagon!
Some dragons are good
Some dragons like wagons, some don't
Some dragons are like other dragons, some aren't
Some dragons like other things
But... All dragons like playing sometimes.

Cariad Krysiak (8)
Staynor Hall Community Primary Academy, Selby

Colourful Space

Space rockets *whooshing!*
Don't fear the dark, although it is tough.
You can see planets of beautiful colours,
You can float around.
You might find space treasure,
But you must be sure.
Legend says there might have been a curse!
There are many myths,
You must be careful, though,
There are floating colours all around.
You might see the sun and moon.

Elliot Shaw (8)
Staynor Hall Community Primary Academy, Selby

Me And The F1 Drivers

Once upon a dream, there was a boy called Harry who was 7 years old in Selby. He was going to pick up Lewis Hamilton, Lando Norris, Charles Leclerc, Carlos Sainz and Sergio Perez. Then we all ran to a rocket ship and we went in and boomed into space. Next, I saw Noah with his dragon who was called Charlie. We got out of the rocket ship and we started racing. I was racing for Ferrari.

Harry Renshaw (7)
Staynor Hall Community Primary Academy, Selby

My Pegasus

My pegasus is helpful,
And says things with such emphasis.
When he does his poo,
It smells like cotton candy.
Want to smell it?
You can fit it in a stable,
And he attends flying lessons,
Because he isn't able to fly just yet.
He has a cat's-eye and will never say goodbye.
Be positive.
Not negative.

Sebastian Lee (8)
Staynor Hall Community Primary Academy, Selby

Friends Forever

I was stuck in a meadow,
Then I saw a fairy,
So we started to be friends,
Then we skipped through the flowers,
And we sang with them.
Then we sat in the sticky, long grass
Together.
Then we skipped back to my home,
Which was built with marshmallows.
It had chocolate cookie walls.

Isabella McCormack (7)
Staynor Hall Community Primary Academy, Selby

All About The Football Match

Once I went to a football stadium. The match was very boring, and the ball had just magically left the stadium, so the players had to find the match ball. At last, they found it and they got back to playing again, and they reached injury time and there was ages left to play, and the players played what they could play.

Patrick Mobbs (8)
Staynor Hall Community Primary Academy, Selby

Gaming Day

I want to game, all day, even at night,
I like gaming to the moon and back,
Gaming is good, it's really fun.
I play Fortnite, Minecraft and Roblox,
Gaming is my thing.
Gaming is so, so fun.
Sometimes I like to rumble tumble down a hill
But all this is just a dream.

William Curtis (7)
Staynor Hall Community Primary Academy, Selby

My Dreams

My dream is to be a singer. My voice can go high and low. I could be an opera singer like many people. I wish to be in a stadium singing as well as playing guitar. Alternatively, I could be a gymnast. I could be anything but my dream is to be a singer. I would be nervous and excited to go on stage.

Lolah Ascough (9)
Staynor Hall Community Primary Academy, Selby

Dinosaurs Went To Space

I was getting ready for bed and brushing my teeth, when that moment I heard a *smashing* and *banging* noise! I looked outside and I saw... dinosaurs! They were flying into space! It was crazy. One is called Rye and he couldn't die, and he liked to eat pie, and he was a spy.

Max Speight (8)
Staynor Hall Community Primary Academy, Selby

Nightmares Of Dread

Every time when I looked out my window
I saw a black cat eating a rat
I hoped it was not a dream but real
I looked around, I saw a bright blue bear
He started to chase me all around the jungle
With a bungle, I saw a snake, not as
Bright as a bite.

Ruby Vincent (8)
Staynor Hall Community Primary Academy, Selby

Spring

Super spring,
Pretty trees and leaves,
Red leaves on the ground.

Imagine all the beautiful leaves on trees;
Hardly, the leaves broke on the floor.

Growing, the leaves on the trees are growing.
I do not know why they are dying.

Toby Hammill (8)
Staynor Hall Community Primary Academy, Selby

Godzilla's Tea Party

Godzilla's tea party is where you want to be in the wreckage of the Star Destroyer. It goes bang, bang, bang. Kong and a teapot that's face is like a demon from the fires of Hell. The teapot grows arms and legs and destroys everything and falls fast asleep.

James Stokoe (9)
Staynor Hall Community Primary Academy, Selby

Flying My...

I'm riding a dragon and I fall off,
And get caught by a bird.
I get chucked into the nest and
Get pecked so hard by the baby birds,
I fly into space and eat the moon;
Because it is cheese.

Kasper Foster (7)
Staynor Hall Community Primary Academy, Selby

Amazing Football

F antastic
O oooh
O ooooh "Goal!"
T reble for Leeds
B allon d'Or
A ll are amazing
L ucky
L ucky oh no football.

Harry Fisher (9)
Staynor Hall Community Primary Academy, Selby

Everything I Love

Chocolate is sweet to eat,
Glitter sparkles in the light,
Pizza is yummy, in my tummy,
Spiders crawl, in their webs.
Dogs bark in the garden,
The beach is warm and fun.

Macauley Pulleyn (8)
Staynor Hall Community Primary Academy, Selby

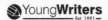

My Dream Dream

D ream
E lephant
A ccomplish
T aylor
H at

S ift
T actical
A ggressive
R abbit.

William Challis (9)
Staynor Hall Community Primary Academy, Selby

My Dream

My dream is to be a
Pro football player and to be good
At trampolining and
In football I can win medals
And a lot more;
And win games
With my team.

Harrison Lister (9)
Staynor Hall Community Primary Academy, Selby

A Football Disaster

F ran Kirby.

O ooh goal!

O hh.

T he fans.

B all.

A lessia Russo.

L ucy Bronze.

L auren Hemp.

Arabella Bradshaw (9)
Staynor Hall Community Primary Academy, Selby

Daydream

Everyone keeps talking about what we have to do,
You're going to Year 6, they say, it will all be something new!

I don't feel like I'm ready; I can barely hold my pen,
Can we have a do-over and learn it all again?

I'm worried for what comes after: the going to big school,
I don't think I'm ready yet; I'm still learning to be cool.

Now I'm thinking about college and buying my first house,
This shouldn't be in my head just yet, I'm still quiet like a mouse.

Mum says not to panic, these things won't happen yet,
Just take each day as it comes; no need to get upset.

So for today, I'm gonna be just a happy kid,
And fall asleep dreaming about playing for Real Madrid.

I like playing with my friends on Xbox, and Dad says that's just fine,
Because growing up will happen one day, but for today I am just nine.

Oliver Keen (9)
Victory Primary School, Portsmouth

I Had A Dream

I had a dream the other day
Right at the beginning of May
I closed my eyes and drifted off
I couldn't hear a thing, not even a moth

It all started with my nan giving me a box
It was shaped sort of like a fox
I lifted the lid and looked inside
Two toys, not thin but wide

The horse was blue with a silver mane
It looked ready to gallop down the lane
The elephant was dainty and pink
Hold on, did it just wink?

We did everything together
"Am I weird?" They said, "Never."
We even played on the trampoline
They always understood what I mean

If I asked for something crazy
It would always come to me
But soon the time came to end the fun
It was getting dark and playtime was done

My eyes soon opened, I realised it was a dream
The best dream I mean
When the dream was dead
I could not wait to go to bed.

Avery Herridge (10)
Victory Primary School, Portsmouth

I Believe In Fairies

Every night,
With my eyes shut tight,
I dream wonderful things;
Fairies with exquisite wings;
Unicorns with dazzling horns;
Gnomes mowing their front lawns.

Then I start to imagine,
A fire-breathing dragon,
A cackling old witch,
An ogre who lives in a ditch.

These horrible things swirled around in my head,
Until I suddenly woke up in bed.
I realised these things weren't real,
But then they came into my room, maybe looking for a meal!

I screamed and screamed,
And suddenly beamed,
Shouted, "I believe in fairies!"
Then they began to get lairy,
But one by one they walked out of my room;
The fire-breathing dragon, the ogre and the witch with the broom.

Hannah Aarons (10)
Victory Primary School, Portsmouth

Twilight Moon Dreams

Dreaming under soft blue twilight moons
With fairies dancing to faraway tunes
A place where memories and fantasies collide
Where playful elves march with pride.

Magical unicorns by a rainbow you'll see
Dead man's fingers reaching up beside trees
Lengthening shadows and toadstools all around
Mischief and mayhem, lots of fun to be found.

Deer prancing around in a settling mist
Dewdrops on flowers settling like a moon's kiss
Jangling bluebells hiding in a haze
A whispered symphony of magical days.

Safe in a meadow surrounded by flowers
I draw up the covers no need to cower
This wonderful place where magic and beauty entwine
These twilight moon dreams are always mine.

Diana Lacey (10)
Victory Primary School, Portsmouth

The Journey

I'm going to take you back in time,
To a place where dinosaurs lived and thrived.
It was millions of years ago,
A place where you would never know.
It was me and my brother and our dog.
The trees were big, full of fog.
We were looking around left and right,
To our surprise, we had a fright.
There was a big T-rex, scary and grey,
He looked at us then looked away.
Before I could think, he took my brother away,
I searched and searched beyond belief,
Until I saw his big white teeth,
I took the stick and pointed at him.
I shouted, "Give me my brother back."
He roared out loud and shook the ground.
He put my brother down and ran away.

Chase Britton (10)
Victory Primary School, Portsmouth

158

Tiny Tigers

Tiny tigers look to the sky,
They wonder why,
Why is the sky so big and vast?
Even in the past I was tiny they thought.
The tiger teacher taught about how big the Earth is.
When my mum gave birth to me I was as tiny as can be.
Tiny tigers began to write down,
And all the tiny tigers had a frown on their faces.
Oh, Earth, why so big, so big and vast,
One day I'll be fast,
And loud and big,
A bug is no match for me.
Years later, tiny tigers became big tigers.
Bigger than bugs and slugs.
Big tigers hunt,
Big tigers have feasts.
I am a beast!
A tiger as some would call me.

Scarlett Page (10)
Victory Primary School, Portsmouth

The Night We Got Trapped In A Nightmare

The night was young
The fresh air slipped into my lungs
These cookie crumbs fell onto my tongue
Suddenly, my head was banging like a drum
I saw a dancer with pleasure and glee
She told me her name was Lee
She told me where to go because I was lost
I felt like frost
Because of the fog
And I saw a frog
A wizard came along and he ponged
Wow, you're a man, I know I have a pen
Zombies are not real
All of us fit in a wheel
Rolling down a hill
Dang! I hit an old mill.

Isla Chappell (10)
Victory Primary School, Portsmouth

Henry's Life

My name was Henry and I had six wives,
They were all very beautiful and lovely brides.

I had three children, two girls and a boy,
Which really gave me such joy.

I became King of England back in my day,
Which was such an achievement as some might say.

Standing over six foot I was really tall,
It made some of my wives look very small!

I'm laid to rest next to my ex-wife,
Now I hope you understand a little about my life.

Ivy Belle Lewis (9)
Victory Primary School, Portsmouth

The Pompey Dream

Saturday afternoon with my dearest dad,
I saw Yengi running, what a lad.
The crowd is screaming,
Mousinho is dreaming.
The future is bright,
It's a perfect night.

As the final whistle blows,
The noise of the fans grows,
Run on the pitch,
Try not to fall into a ditch.

Pack lifts the cup,
Fratton Park, it's time to erupt.
Super Pompey going up!

Lenny Bull (10)
Victory Primary School, Portsmouth

Mr Bailey

M y teacher is Mr Bailey

R ules is what he likes in his classroom, he's

B onkers about his PS4 even though Xbox is way better

A s annoying as he can be

I enjoy being in his class and getting to

L augh at him while he is dressed as

E lsa, he sings, 'Let It Go'. He thinks he is

Y oung, even though everyone calls him old.

Alfie Brown (10)
Victory Primary School, Portsmouth

Out Of This World

S oaring above Earth, no one to be seen, all on my own, just me and my thoughts.

P recious Earth so pretty and bright.

A ll of the colours stand out just right, all around the atmosphere, creates a bubble of life.

C overing the Earth with shining light, oh how the stars shine so bright.

E arth that we call home, surely we can't be alone.

Joshua Irons (10)
Victory Primary School, Portsmouth

Dreaming Rulers

In my marvellous dreams,
I see many rulers that were supreme.
They teach me many facts,
Even all the attacks.

Queen Victoria taught me about Victorians,
Some of it was not known by historians.

So did Henry VIII,
All about the Tudor faiths,

That was the end of my dream,
I wake up, and my eyes gleam.

Piper Hartley (10)
Victory Primary School, Portsmouth

My Family

My family is the best,
When I go in my house I feel like it is a family nest.
I have loving people by my side,
Even if they don't smile wide.

My family is all I need,
Even if I am just a little seed.
I hate when I fight with my brother,
And no one succeeds,
We should care,
We are here for each other.

Elise East (9)
Victory Primary School, Portsmouth

Poems

P oems are good, poems are great, poems are brilliant.

O f course I love poems, they are just so good.

E very single poem, every single line, every single syllable.

M y favourite poem is... well I don't know, I love them all!

S o if you love poems, we'll explore the world of poetry!

Cody Jenkins (10)

Victory Primary School, Portsmouth

Untitled

In the goal, I stood so tall
Ready to catch the speeding ball
With gloves so big and me so brave
I make the save,
I make the save.

Jumping high and diving low
I'm quick and strong, just watch me go
For every kick and every cheer
The goal is safe because I'm here.

Riley Duffett (10)
Victory Primary School, Portsmouth

In My Dreams

In my dreams,
I fly through the sky,
I dive,
I loop the loop,
I fight against the monsters!
Then shoot a fire blast so big.
Then I'd eject into thin air!
But when I wake up,
I'm tired and frail,
And then I can't get up!
I wonder why?

Miguel Senobua (10)
Victory Primary School, Portsmouth

Midnight Forest

In my dreams, every night,
Fairies invite me to their castle,
Where they eat lettuce,
And play tennis.
One of the fairies is called Lola,
The other is called Pola,
They love their castle,
But when it turns midnight,
Strange things are seen on site.

Poppy McMillan (10)
Victory Primary School, Portsmouth

The Flower Garden

The flowers bloom all day,
The children run around and play,
The trees stand so proud and high.
It is beautiful, I cannot lie.
When I see the butterflies,
It makes me feel alive.
The beautiful trees,
Sway peacefully in the breeze.

Amelia Ellis (10)
Victory Primary School, Portsmouth

Losing A Loved One

Losing a loved one is not fair
For the people who loved and cared
Just in the sky, in the air
Looking upon us with a loving stare
Please come down and give me a hand
I'm struggling so much
Please come down, I miss your touch.

Eli Hollis (10)
Victory Primary School, Portsmouth

Manchester City

M aths

A poem

N ever school for life

C are for family

H ouse is important

E ver life

S ame as always

T eamwork

E xcellence

R espect for Man City.

Taiten-Ray Holden (10)

Victory Primary School, Portsmouth

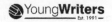

Portsmouth Championship

They have made the win happen,
Come on Pompey, let's go,
Championship,
Come on Pompey,
To the Premier League,
To the Champions League,
Let's go, Pompey,
Let's go,
For a go.

Sebastian Marsh (9)
Victory Primary School, Portsmouth

Superpowers

I had a dog
His name was Bog
Bog had a superpower
Not just any ordinary power
It's the smelly poo
When he takes a poo
I say boo
It goes everywhere
So we give him underwear!

Calum Smith (10)
Victory Primary School, Portsmouth

My Worst Nightmare

A new holiday...
We had neighbours,
They had twin sisters and they were mad.
They made a chant,
Lay was pushed into a wormhole,
And so was my family,
They felt bad so they said sorry.

Lilly Barton (10)
Victory Primary School, Portsmouth

My Cat

My cat has a hat
And she is lying on a mat
But then the magic happened
A brightened light turned on
It was the hat... on the cat
And then the hat flew away.

Eva Udy (10)
Victory Primary School, Portsmouth

Milo

Milo is a nice but annoying dog
He eats, sleeps but doesn't stop
He steals stuff
He eats toys
But he is so loving.

Jayden Nutland (9)
Victory Primary School, Portsmouth

The Boy Who Bullied People

I am the bully
The rude bully
The one who bullies another bully
And I am rude to everyone I know.

George Jeune (9)
Victory Primary School, Portsmouth

YOUNG WRITERS INFORMATION

We hope you have enjoyed reading this book – and that you will continue to in the coming years.

If you're a young writer who enjoys reading and creative writing, or the parent of an enthusiastic poet or story writer, do visit our website **www.youngwriters.co.uk**. Here you will find free competitions, workshops and games, as well as recommended reads, a poetry glossary and our blog.

If you would like to order further copies of this book, or any of our other titles, then please give us a call or visit **www.youngwriters.co.uk**.

Young Writers
Remus House
Coltsfoot Drive
Peterborough
PE2 9BF
(01733) 890066
info@youngwriters.co.uk

f YoungWritersUK   ✕ YoungWritersCW
📷 youngwriterscw   ♪ youngwriterscw